"Lilies...some of the most stately and beautiful of garden flowers..." Lilium
Regale in a formal garden setting.

LILIES FOR ENGLISH GARDENS.

A GUIDE FOR AMATEURS.

BY

GERTRUDE JEKYLL.

ANTIQUE COLLECTORS' CLUB

ISBN 0 907462 28 6

First published by Country Life/George Newnes Ltd., 1901.
This edition published for the Antique Collectors' Club by
the Antique Collectors' Club Ltd. 1982, with 8 colour
illustrations added.

British Library CIP Data
Jekyll, Gertrude
    Lilies for English gardens
    1. Lilies
    I. Title
    625.9'34324   SB413.L7

Printed in England by Baron Publishing, Woodbridge, Suffolk

H20 499 174 ✗

CONTENTS

5

CONTENTS

INTRODUCTION

LILIES, comprising as they do, some of the most stately and beautiful of garden flowers, are not nearly so much grown in gardens as their beauty deserves. One may go through many a rather large place and not see a Lily from one end to the other, and in spite of the enormous and ever-increasing interest in gardens and flowers of these days, a large proportion of the people who are taking a practical interest in horticulture hardly as yet know one Lily from another.

The present writer and compiler, who has been a working amateur for thirty years, has keenly felt the want of a short, concise, illustrated handbook ; such a book as will just tell amateurs in the plainest way what they are most likely to want to know about Lilies. Such a book has therefore been prepared in the form of the present volume, in which the information has been condensed and put as shortly as possible for greater simplicity and ease of reference.

Early in 1900 the editors of *The Garden*, feeling that it was desirable to encourage the growth of these good plants, sent out circulars to some thirty known growers of Lilies, in order to ascertain firstly what

Lilies were the easiest of general culture, and secondly in what circumstances various other Lilies might be considered successful in different parts of the United Kingdom. The result of these inquiries is herewith published, with acknowledgments to those who so readily and courteously complied with the request.

Acknowledgments are also due to Mr. W. Robinson for permission to make reproductions of Lily portraits from some of the former *Garden* plates; to several friends of *The Garden*, especially to Miss Willmott, Mr. G. F. Wilson, and Messrs. Wallace of Colchester, for photographs of Lilies, and to Mr. E. T. Cook, joint-editor of *The Garden*, for much helpful advice and assistance.

It must be understood that this is merely an amateur's handbook; a simple guide to those who wish to grow Lilies in English gardens. Several Lilies known to exist are not named in it, either because they are of secondary importance in our gardens or because they are scarce or tender or little known. They concern the botanist, whose business it is to know and to classify everything; they scarcely concern the gardener whose interest it is to know what Lilies will best grace his garden.

The Lilies named are (with grateful acknowledgment to the work of that eminent botanist) arranged according to the classification of Mr. J. G. Baker, so long Keeper of the Herbarium and Library of the Royal Gardens at Kew.

A careful observation of the distinctive features of the great divisions of Lilies will not only give additional ·interest to the plants themselves, but will give the amateur grower some grasp of the botanical aspect, by helping him to observe the evidences of the common laws of structure that have been accepted in determining the relationships of the groups. No one could believe, who has not taken the trouble to learn these simple and now plainly defined characters, how the possession of such knowledge increases our interest in any group of plants. What a joy it is, in Daffodils for instance, to have acquired a " Daffodil eye," so that when any new Narcissus, whether collected wild or produced by intentional hybridisation, is shown, to be able at a glance to guess fairly nearly at its parentage and quite surely at its clanship. In the matter of Lilies it is much easier, for the forms in the several groups are more distinct.

In addition to the acknowledgment so justly due to Mr. Baker, it would be ungracious on the part of any one venturing to put together a handbook on Lilies to omit some grateful reference to the labours of others who have worked among these noble flowers; to the travels and writings of Mr. Henry Elwes, author of the " Monograph," the standard authority on Lilies; to the many years of experiment and written record of Mr. G. F. Wilson; and to the industry and perseverance of Mr. Max Leichtlin of Baden-Baden.

Perhaps it is to Mr. Wilson above all that amateurs are mostly indebted, for his untiring work during the last thirty years in large and long-continued practical trials, and for his unwearied kindness in allowing all who desired instruction to see the results ; also for his generosity in communicating at once to the horticultural press anything about Lilies that he perceived to be of educational value.

LILIUM RUBELLUM; DELICATE PINK; (Three inches across.)

LILIES FOR ENGLISH GARDENS

CHAPTER I

LILIES AS CLASSIFIED

THE genus Lilium is, according to Mr. Baker's classification, divided into six subgenera, of which five especially concern our gardens.

Sub-genus I. is called *Cardiocrinum.*
This has only two species, of which the best is *Lilium giganteum.* It has white, funnel - shaped flowers, and, unlike other Lilies, wide heart-shaped leaves, much like Arum leaves, on long stalks.

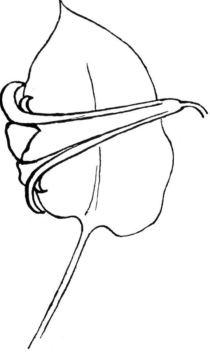

L. GIGANTEUM.

13

Sub-genus II. is called *Eulirion*.

The flowers in this are also funnel-shaped, but the leaves are long, either with their sides parallel (linear)

L. CANDIDUM.

or of some length, thickest in the middle and tapering at both ends (lanceolate). This comprises among other Lilies, *longiflorum*, *candidum*, *japonicum* (otherwise *Brownii*), and *Krameri*.

Sub-genus III. is called *Archelirion*.

The flower is of a very open funnel-shape, and its divisions are widely spread, and a little turned back.

L. SPECIOSUM.

The central style or pistil comes forward in a boldly curved line, and the stamens, instead of accompanying it more or less as in some other Lilies, diverge from it all round, giving the flower a distinct aspect. The leaves are either without stalk (sessile), or have the stalk very short. This sub-genus includes *tigrinum, auratum, speciosum,* and perhaps the newer *Henryi.*

Sub-genus IV. is called *Isolirion.*

In this sub-genus the flower is an open cup of orange, or reddish-orange colouring carried upright, such as the Orange Lily (*L. croceum*).

L. CROCEUM.

Sub-genus V. is called *Martagon.*

These are Lilies of more or less turn-cap or turk's-cap shape ; *L. canadense,* which is bell-shaped, being the most notable exception. About half of them have the leaves in whorls. The purple *Martagon* and the scarlet *chalcedonicum* are the commonest represen-tatives among garden Lilies.

Sub-genus VI. is called *Notholirion.*

This sub-genus is not here considered, as it is a link with the Fritillaries, L. MARTAGON.

and the only two species it contains are difficult and by no means indispensable garden flowers.

CHAPTER II

SUB-GENUS I

LILIUM GIGANTEUM (Eastern Himalayas), *Cardiocrinum*

THE great beauty and surprising dimensions of the giant Lily well repay the trouble needed for its cultivation. Though a true Lily, its wide, succulent leaves have almost the appearance of those of a giant Arum.

In cool woodland, in a light, loamy soil, it can easily be grown; indeed there are woods in England where it grows so readily that it may be said to have become naturalised, growing spontaneously from self-sown seed. But in most gardens and home woodlands it is thankful for well-prepared holes of light sandy loam with leaf-mould and enrichment of well-decayed manure.

The root is unlike that of most Lilies, for instead of consisting of whitish or yellowish scales, only adhering by their bases, it is a solid bulb of dark bottle-green colour, shaped something like an oil-flask with a shortened neck. It makes no stem roots,[1] all its root-growth coming from the bulb, and radiating

[1] See page 139

LILIUM GIGANTEUM; (*Tallest spike 11ft. 6ins.*)

laterally only a little way underground. The roots look like those of a young tree or the great spreading ones of *Eremurus robustus*. The flowering stems have need of these great roots, for they rise to a height of from ten to fourteen feet, though they are perhaps best at from ten to eleven feet. In the last days of June, or the earliest days of July, the great trumpet-shaped flowers expand, each eight to nine inches long, and four or five inches across the mouth. They are greenish-yellow when they begin to open, but pure white when fully opened, when they show a red-purple band inside. The great stem bears from twelve to twenty, or even more, of these flowers within some two feet of the top.

The fragrance is powerful and delicious, and carries far in the still summer evenings when the light is waning, at which time these grand Lilies look their best.

Planted bulbs, unless quite full-sized, do not flower for two or three years ; indeed it is much better that they should not do so, but that they should slowly grow and gather strength. The flower coming the next year on a large-sized bulb is rarely a good one, and it is better, unless it promises unusual vigour, to remove it and let the bulb grow and strengthen. Unless seed is wanted, it is best for the bulb to remove the upper part of the flower-stem after blooming, as this will help the offsets, although it is a handsome object all the summer, retaining its leaves and its polished greenness, while the large upturned pods are fine things also.

Lilium Giganteum Cardiocrinum. "*The fragrance is powerful and delicious, and carries far in the still summer evenings when the light is waning, at which time these grand Lilies look their best.*"

If good seed is wanted, it is well to insure it by repeated hand-fertilisation. Increase by seed is rather a slow process, as flowering bulbs can hardly be expected till seven years from the time of sowing.

The plant that has flowered will have offsets of several sizes, the largest of which will probably flower in two years. The bulbs are planted quite shallow, only just underground; established ones show their tops just above ground.

In most gardens, though it does not appear to be needed everywhere, care must be taken that the young leaves do not suffer from late frosts. In the neighbourhood of London, and for some way to the south of that latitude, the young leafy growths need to be protected by a few Fir boughs, or something that will "break" the frost without so closely covering the Lilies as to draw and weaken them.

Lilium cordifolium of Japan may be described as a poor kind of *L. giganteum*, and is so inferior to this grand thing, that unless it is an object to have a collection of as many kinds as may be, it is hardly worth growing.

*LILIUM GIGANTEUM; WHITE, WITH RED-PURPLE STRIPE
INSIDE (Flowers ten inches long).*

LILIUM LONGIFLORUM; WHITE; (Six inches long by five inches wide.)

CHAPTER III

SUB-GENUS II

LILIUM LONGIFLORUM (Japan), *Eulirion*
Bermuda Lily

THIS most beautiful Japanese Lily appears in our
gardens under the various names of *Harrisi, eximium,
Wilsoni,* and *grandiflorum.* These are all good garden
varieties of the same plant. The white trumpet
flowers, borne one or two on a stem in the type
plant, but more numerously in the stronger kinds,
have yellow anthers that help to give the flower an
appearance of great purity, while its fine build gives
an impression of consummate beauty of Lily form.

An immense quantity are grown in Japan for ex-
portation, so that the moderate price at which it
may be bought is an encouragement to free planting.

The fine variety *Wilsoni* is a plant of great vigour,
often bearing six or eight flowers on a stem ; *grandiflorum* is also a very fine Lily.

The name Bermuda Lily is somewhat misleading,
for the plant is Japanese. But as it was found to
increase readily and mature more quickly in the
Bermuda Islands, it was largely grown there under
the name *Harrisi.* It is a Lily that accommodates

itself readily to forcing, and will bear both pushing on early and also retarding.

The bulbs are not of much use after forcing, but they may be turned out and clumped together in some retired spot and given a good watering, when they may give some useful flowers for cutting towards the end of autumn.

When planted out of doors *Lilium longiflorum* cannot be depended upon to prosper and form strong clumps as so many Lilies will do, although it forms young bulbs on the underground stem and by the breaking up of the old bulbs. These can be collected and grown on, but it is hardly worth doing in private gardens. Still if it is desired to do so the separated scales may be put rather thickly in pans and grown on in the greenhouse.

This grand Lily is also very useful grown in pots for many outdoor purposes. Nothing is better for dropping into empty spaces, pot and all, in the latter part of the summer, or for standing in any place where pot plants are grouped with foliage plants, a way of gardening that is not half enough considered or practised. In such places it is beautiful in shade, though if kept moist at the root the flower will bear plenty of sun. But its beauty and purity are best enjoyed in a shaded position.

It should be planted six to seven inches deep, as it forms stem roots, or if in pots, should be in deep-shaped pots and potted low, so that additional soil of a rich compost can be added for the nourishment of the upper set of roots.

A FIELD OF LILIUM LONGIFLORUM IN MESSRS BOEHMER'S GROUNDS, JAPAN

LILIUM LONGIFLORUM; WHITE (Six inches long by five inches wide.) ANTHERS YELLOW.

PART OF A FIELD OF L. LONGIFLORUM IN JAPAN.

LILIUM NEILGHERRENSE; CREAM COLOURED, FAINTLY
PURPLE OUTSIDE. (*Flowers Six inches.*)

LILIUM NEPALENSE; CITRON AND PURPLE; (Flowers Four inches wide.)

LILIUM LOWI ; WHITE, SPOTTED RED PURPLE, RIBS A DELICATE
GREEN SHOWING FAINTLY GREEN TO THE INSIDE
(Flowers Three-and-a-half inches long by four inches wide.)

LILIUM PHILIPPINENSE; WHITE; YELLOW ANTHERS;
(Eight inches long, by five inches wide.)

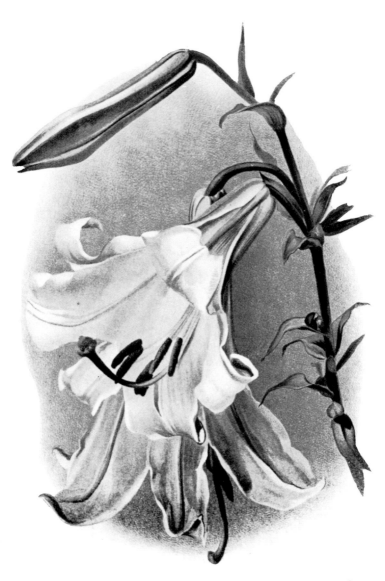

*LILIUM SULPHUREUM; WHITE, YELLOW INSIDE; RIBS
ROSY; ANTHERS DEEP ORANGE.* (Flowers Six
inches long by Five inches across.)

A compost of light loam and leaf-mould will suit it, and it is advised to stimulate rather with small doses of such a dressing as nitrate of soda than with ordinary manure.

LILIUM NEILGHERRENSE (NILGHIRIS), *Eulirion*
L. NEPALENSE (NEPAUL), *Eulirion*
L. LOWI (BURMA), *Eulirion*
L. PHILIPPINENSE (PHILIPPINES), *Eulirion*
L. SULPHUREUM, SYN. WALLICHIANUM (BURMA), *Eulirion*

These Oriental Lilies are not to be considered hardy in England, though *L. nepalense* and *L. sulphureum* have been successfully flowered out of doors in Devonshire. But they are noble plants in the greenhouse. In their great solidity of substance and grand texture, purity of white and tender tinting of yellow and pinkish colouring, they have been found to be admirable plants for cool greenhouse treatment.

L. neilgherrense does well in a mixture of equal parts of loam and peat with a good proportion of silver sand. The massive funnel-shaped flower is usually of a creamy white colour, sometimes faintly tinted outside with purple. It has a sweet scent quite peculiar to itself. Like other Lilies that have a solid waxy texture, the bloom lasts long. It flowers in autumn.

L. nepalense succeeds in the same conditions. The flower is yellow or almost greenish, with purple centre.

L. philippinense is a graceful plant with a drooping, pure white trumpet eight inches long and six inches wide at the mouth.

L. sulphureum is a noble Lily of massive texture, the flower seven inches long and as much wide. It is hardy in our best climates.

L. Lowi has beautiful, white, drooping flowers.

Those who wish to cultivate these tender Lilies should see them as they are grown in the Himalayan house at Kew, where they are planted out in the borders among the Rhododendrons and Camellias. Here they are more at their ease than in pots, especially *L. neilgherrense*, which has a way of throwing out the flower-spike horizontally on leaving the bulb and before rising out of the ground.

LILIUM CANDIDUM (Southern Europe),
Eulirion
The White Lily, or Madonna Lily

If one might have only one Lily in the garden, it would have to be the beautiful old White Lily that has been with us since the end of the sixteenth century. Although we may take it to be the oldest of its kind in cultivation, we do not by any means know all about its wants and ways. For of all Lilies known in gardens

LILIUM CANDIDUM; WHITE. (*Four inches across.*)   *THE BEST GARDEN FORM.*

it is what is called the most capricious. When we say a plant is capricious, it is, of course, a veiled confession of ignorance, for whereas we may well believe that the laws that govern the well-being of any plant are more or less fixed, and with most plants we can make sure of the right way of culture ; in the case of this Lily we cannot find out what those laws are ; and though it has been more than three hundred years in our gardens, we can only give general advice as to where and how it will do well.

A plant so lovely should be tried in every garden. It may be assumed as a general rule that where the soil is of loam, or of anything rich and holding, whether of a clayey or of a calcareous nature, that there it is likely to do well. Further than that we dare not go, for it is impossible to give a general prescription on several points of culture, such as whether to plant deep or shallow, whether to divide often or to let alone, whether to manure or not ; for, as the result of searching inquiry, we only get the most confusing and contradictory reports from persons whose observations are keen and accurate and whose statements may be accepted as absolutely trustworthy.

Thus, one good gardener says, " In every instance it resented manurial treatment in heavy soils." While another says, " Plant in rich soil well manured." Another, " *L. candidum* likes plenty of manure." As to soil, one writer says, " I think our dry, open soil, saturated with iron, is the cause of bulbs being so healthy." Another says, " In a hot, dry, old garden on a slope, the old Madonna Lily luxuriates ; the rock

"The greater number of the Lilies look their best when seen among shrubs and green growths of handsome foliage. Their forms are so distinct as well as beautiful that they are much best in separate groups among quiet greenery." Lilium Enchantment with Lilum Regale.

LILIUM CANDIDUM; THE LESS GOOD FORM, NOT FULLY EXPANDED.

THE WHITE LILY IN THE GARDEN LANDSCAPE

THE WHITE LILY IN A GARDEN IN VENICE.

is limestone, and there is a good deal of umber in the ground." On the other hand, the highest authority says, " As to shade, we observe vigorous and healthy specimens of *L. candidum* growing year after year in a shady position," and "*L. candidum* likes general shade from buildings or trees." Then from the Riviera we are told that they are " planted nine inches deep in sandy soil exposed to the burning summer heat." A distinguished amateur in Kent says, " Few things have stood heat and drought so well as this Lily."

Then again we are told, " In the heavy marsh land, with water very near the surface—a heavy clay that bakes hard in summer—the White Lily flourishes." In Berkshire, where at the great house the gardener could not grow White Lilies, they were grand in a near cottage (one of two) side by side, and failures in the next. The goodwife accounted for her flourishing Lilies by saying that whereas her neighbour left the Lilies dry, she watered hers copiously.

Then as to replanting ; one says, " Let alone four or five years " ; another, " Lift and divide every other year, and replant in fresh ground." On the Berkshire chalk downs an informant says, " They have not been touched for twelve or fourteen years." From the South of France a successful grower writes, " They have never been moved." Another at home says, " Never disturb, but give a yearly top-dressing of rich compost" ; and another, " I have known them undisturbed for twenty years."

The lesson taught by all these contradictions is, that every one must try how to grow the White Lily in his

WHITE LILY IN A GARDEN BORDER ; THE BEST OR WIDE-PETALLED FORM

THE THINNER OR STARRY FORM OF THE WHITE LILY.

GROUP OF WHITE LILY.

WHITE LILY IN A GARDEN BORDER: THE BEST FORM.

LILIUM BROWNII IN A DEVON GARDEN.

LILIUM JAPONICUM BROWNII. PURE WHITE, RED-BROWN OUTSIDE;
ANTHERS RED-BROWN (*Width Five-and-a-half inches.*)

THE WHITE LILY WITH OTHER FLOWERS IN THE GARDEN BORDER.

THE WHITE LILY IN A THAMES VALLEY GARDEN.

own garden. If it does well, let it alone till it shows signs of deterioration. Try some in manured ground, and some in the natural soil; some in sun, and some in shade; some watered, some left dry. For their general health it may be assumed that a sheltered place, where the Lilies would be protected from biting winds, will generally suit them best, for it has been observed that where the dreaded Lily disease attacks them, those that were partly sheltered by shrubs and trees escaped, while the ones in the open were destroyed.

There are two forms of the White Lily; the less good one thin and starry, with petals not much turned back, the better one with broad, stoutly ribbed petals strongly recurved.

For replanting most Lilies, the rule is to do it as soon as the leaves turn yellow, but the best growers advise, in the case of *L. candidum*, to replant before this, soon after the flowers are over and before the leaves show any signs of yellowing.

LILIUM JAPONICUM, syn. L. ODORUM (Japan),
Eulirion

Of this genus the Lily that most concerns our gardens is the strong variety, *L. japonicum Brownii*, commonly known as *Lilium Brownii*. This grand Lily stands three or four feet high and bears from one to four of its massive fragrant flowers of pure white colour and trumpet shape on a stem that curves gracefully and is well clothed with handsome foliage, persisting after the flower is over. The outside of the flower is heavily coloured with purplish-brown, and the conspicuous deep brown rust-coloured anthers add to the appearance of purity of the inside of the flower. There is a variety known as *leucanthemum* which is white outside as well as in.

It is a grand plant for light soils in the South of England, and loves a sheltered but warm place. There are not many Lilies that like a light sandy soil, but this fine kind is content with almost pure sand with a little manure. It is so grown by the Dutch nurserymen, and also largely in the sandy soils near Berlin. It does not refuse to grow in stiffer land, for we hear of its doing well in the strong red loam of Devonshire, and in heavy soil much farther north. The Japanese plant the bulb on its side in order that winter wet may not lodge among the scales, and in cold heavy soils it would be well to lay something over it to shoot off the wet in winter.

L. Brownii makes roots from the stem as well as from the bulb and should therefore be planted rather deeply, not less than seven inches.

LILIUM KRAMERI (JAPAN), *Eulirion*

This is one of the few pink Lilies of our gardens, and a very lovely thing it is. The flowers are carried horizontally on stems from three to four feet high. The soil generally advised for it is a light loam, but an amateur who grows Lilies with great success in Devonshire says the colour is finest in peat.

*LILIUM JAPONICUM BROWNII IN THE EDGE OF A WOOD AT
MR. WILSON'S.*

LILIUM KRAMERI: PINK: (Six inches.)

LILIUM RUBELLUM.

Lilies "that have scarlet and orange flowers... are admirable in combination with many other garden flowers in the mixed border and various garden spaces." Lilium Miss Willmot.

It is a Lily so beautiful and of a colour so lovely and unusual that it is worth taking pains with. It roots from the stem as well as from the bulb, and therefore should be planted rather deep, fully six to eight inches. It has been known to give as many as seven blooms to one stem, though one flower to a stem is usual.

LILIUM RUBELLUM (JAPAN), *Eulirion*

Of later introduction from Japan is *L. rubellum,* a pink Lily something like a small *Krameri.* Messrs. Wallace of Colchester, who introduced this Lily and distributed it last season, sent me bulbs for trial and advised planting it in sandy soil. It has done admirably, and though so lately introduced is already rising rapidly in favour. It generally bears three of its charming, clear-cut, pink flowers on a stem about a foot high. It seems to be perfectly hardy, and promises to be a Lily for everybody. It flowers early in June.

Mr. Wilson's recent experience of this Lily is described in the following words :—" I think *Lilium rubellum* will become a good garden favourite. As we were desirous to ascertain the best way to grow this Lily, I got a number of imported bulbs and planted them in lots of ten or more in very many situations, and under very different conditions, in October 1899. The result is that we found a mixture of vegetable soil and loam, and a partially shaded situation, was what suited them best.

"Some clumps were planted in deep shade of a wood, some others in partial shade. Both bloomed thoroughly well, but those with most light had the highest colour."

LILIUM PARRYI (CALIFORNIA), *Eulirion*

A pale yellow Lily of great beauty; a plant for cool damp peat, though it has been found to do well in peaty, well-drained soil that has but little moisture.

The pale citron colour is very beautiful, and the slender stem, four to six feet high, carries the graceful hanging flowers, with their conspicuous brown anthers, on stalks from four to six inches long.

The root is not a round bulb, but is inclined to be rhizomatous, though not so distinctly so as in another American Lily, *L. pardalinum*. It has a delicate and delicious scent, not unlike that of *auratum*, but less heavy and overpowering.

This Lily has not as yet been much grown; a highly favourable account of it from a careful amateur in Kent should be an encouragement to try it in all gardens where the suitable conditions of peat and moisture can be obtained.

Mr. Carl Purdy says *L. Parryi* is not a bog plant. Its home in California is at an elevation of from seven to ten thousand feet, near streams and in alpine meadows, in a soil two-thirds granitic sand and one-third peat or mould.

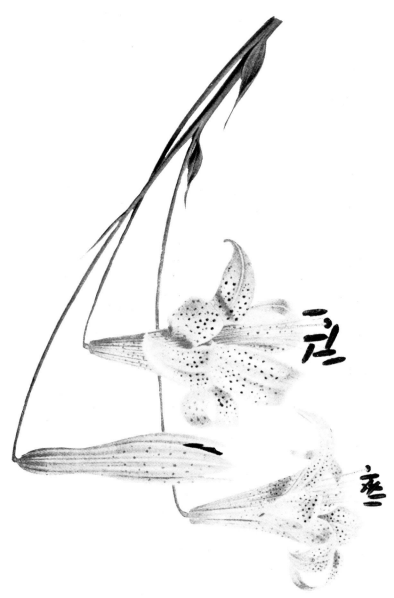

LILIUM PARRYI; PORTION OF A SPIKE LIFE-SIZE. COLOUR CITRON, ANTHERS DEEP ORANGE.

LILIUM WALLACEI; SALMON ORANGE;
(Five-and-a-half inches wide, by Two-and-a-half inches long.)

LILIUM WASHINGTONIANUM (California),
Eulirion

A beautiful Lily, with fragrant drooping white flowers on a stem about four feet high. The back of the flower has a lilac tinge. There is a shorter-stemmed variety known as *purpureum*, whose whole flower is of a purplish colour when mature. We hear of *L. washingtonianum* doing well in loam in Norfolk near the sea, and in Northumberland in strong loam on a clay subsoil. The variety *rubescens* is recommended as a vigorous kind with a pinkish flower. It is not yet much grown but probably has a good future.

LILIUM WALLACEI (Japan), *Eulirion*

A very handsome Lily, flowering late; of a beautiful colour, like the warmest apricot but more rosy. It likes a damp place. It is of Japanese origin and is said to be a garden hybrid.

CHAPTER IV

SUB-GENUS III

LILIUM TIGRINUM (China), *Archelirion*
Tiger Lily

THOUGH introduced from China not much more than a hundred years ago, the Tiger Lily is among those that we cherish as old English garden flowers, so familiar is it, not only in our gardens, but in old pictures and in the samplers and embroideries of our great-grandmothers.

Excepting the later blooms of *L. auratum*, some of which go on till the end of October, the Tiger is the latest flowering of our Lilies, being in full bloom in September. Its bold, turn-cap form is so well known that it can want no description, except to draw attention to its remarkable colour, a soft salmon-orange, that can be matched by but few other flowers, nearest perhaps by some of the Cape bulbs, such as Homeria collina, and one of the Ixias. The black spots and dark stems and deep-brown, rust-coloured anthers combine to make a grand garden flower.

It is about the only Lily that we have in a good double form, for though there is a so-called double *L. candidum*, it is a wretched, misshapen thing, not worth growing.

PART OF A SPIKE OF L. TIGRINUM SPLENDENS; SALMON;
(Five inches.)

LILIUM AURATUM: WHITE WITH YELLOW (SOMETIMES ROSE-COLOURED) STRIPE ON THE INSIDE OF THE PETALS, AND CHOCOLATE SPOTS: (Flowers Six to Ten inches wide; plant from Five to Ten feet high)

There are several good forms of Tiger Lily besides the old ordinary one, which is always a capital garden plant. *L. Fortunei* is a bold plant, and the most woolly of the tomentose kinds. There is a still larger one, known as *Fortunei giganteum.* The flowers of these are of a paler colour than the type, and the stems are greener.

Leopoldi is a variety whose stems are dark and smooth. But the finest of all is the one known as *splendens*, with the largest flowers of the strongest colour, sometimes growing to a height of seven feet.

Bulbs of the Tiger Lilies should be planted rather deep, about seven inches, as they have stem-roots. They increase fairly fast, and should be replanted about every three years. They can also be readily increased by the abundant bulbils that most of them produce in the axils of the leaves. These make flowering bulbs in from three to four years.

It likes a lightish loam, or loamy sand, and leaf-mould, and, like all Lilies, is thankful for a manurial mulch.

LILIUM AURATUM (JAPAN), *Archelirion*
THE GOLD-RAYED LILY OF JAPAN

This is one of the noblest, and in certain circumstances one of the easiest to grow of all Lilies, being grand in cool woodland where it is moist at the root. It is wild in Japan, but when there cultivated for export it is grown on land slightly raised above the flooded rice-fields and on the foot-hills not far from water. Well-sheltered, half-shaded spots in a moist, peaty wood are what it likes best, but, given the necessary condition of shelter (for exposure to cold winds invites disease), and the desirable one of half-shade, it can be grown in well-prepared holes in other soils. These holes may with advantage be four to six feet deep, filled with a mixture of peat and sand, or sandy loam, leaf-mould, and rubbish-heap burnings, with some well-rotted manure.

Where there is no woodland adjoining the garden, an excellent place to grow these Lilies is in Rhododendron or Azalea beds, or any bed where the soil is cool and peaty, and where the young growths will be protected by something bushy. In exposed gardens they suffer from the May frosts. They must not, of course, be actually smothered by the protecting bushes, but they will still do quite well, and make their way through, when the branches of the adjoining bushes first meet.

If the root is cool the top will bear much more sunshine, but the shaded, woody spots are where it looks best.

This grand Lily well planted and left alone for three years will probably then be at its best; after this the bulbs will be likely to have increased so much that it will be well to divide them.

Field mice are mischievous enemies, eating off the tops of the young shoots when they are a few inches out of the ground. Sometimes one may see naked-topped stems rising a foot or two with the leafy top gone. This damage may generally be attributed to

LILIUM AURATUM AMONG RHODODENDRONS AT THE
EDGE OF WOODLAND.

the mice. In this case or that of any other injury the bulb is not necessarily the worse. Many Lilies seem to accept such injury quite philosophically, and devote the energy which has been checked above ground to storing a year's additional strength in the bulb, which will throw up a still finer flowering stem next year.

There are some very fine garden varieties of this grand Lily. The one named *Auratum platyphyllum* is of great size and vigour, the blooms handsomely spotted, and sometimes as much as a foot across; a fine variety of this, called *platyphyllum virginale*, has a yellow band in each division and pale yellow spots. *Rubro-vittatum* has a red band to each petal, and *Wittei* has a flower of great beauty, all white without spots.

Auratum is one of the Lilies that, in addition to the roots that issue from the bulb, has other roots at the base of the stem. It should therefore be planted deeply, even as much as from six to ten inches, in order to insure that the upper rooting system, which nourishes the growing stem, should be well under-ground. In addition to deep planting, a surface mulching of rotten manure, to keep the ground cool and give nutriment, and frequent watering, both to supply moisture and to wash in the goodness of the mulch, are desirable for the welfare of the plants.

This fine Lily is handsome at a height of from six to eight feet, though this is by no means the limit of its stature. It bears from three to thirty flowers on a stem, but is most beautiful when the number of blooms borne is not so great as to crowd the head. It is unusually liable to fasciation, that curious natural freak whereby a number of flower-stems are joined into one, usually of a flattened shape, and a crowded head of a large number of flowers is produced at the top.

LILIUM SPECIOSUM (JAPAN), *Archelirion*

This beautiful Lily is deservedly one of the greatest favourites, for though not often grown in the open border (where also it should be in every good garden), yet it is so amenable to pot culture that it has been largely used in that way, and has meanwhile been somewhat overlooked as a border plant. The name *lancifolium*, by which this Lily has been erroneously called, is one of the synonyms of *L. elegans*.

The flowers of the species within this sub-genus *Archelirion*, are all of daring as well as beautiful form ; the petals are well rolled back, and are handsomely spotted, and often banded with distinct colour. The style is thrown out in a curved line of much grace and strength ; the stamens, instead of following the line of the style as in most other Lilies, boldly diverge from it; the anthers, thickly covered with bright red rust-coloured pollen, are conspicuous from their size and colour and extremely delicate poise. *L. speciosum* has all these attractive qualities, and in addition has a strongly waved outline to the petal, which adds much to its beauty. The markings take the form not only of colour, but, near the centre of the flower, of delicate projecting teeth or bristles ; both words quite inade-

LILIUM SPECIOSUM VAR. MELPOMENE; PINK FLUSHED ROSE.
(Five-and-a-half inches across.)

LILIUM HENRYI: APRICOT ORANGE:
(*Flowers three-and-three-quarter inches across.*)

quately conveying the idea of what is a dainty adornment of a lovely flower.

There are many varieties of this grand Lily. Pure white, faintly flushed with rosy pink, and several of deep rose colour and crimson. *Album novum* and *Album Krætzeri* are beautiful whites, *macranthum*, *Melpomene*, and *roseum superbum* have fine rose and crimson colouring.

It flowers through the late summer and into autumn, and is one of the best of Lilies to arrange in succession to *longiflorum*. For pot culture the Lilies should be repotted when they have turned yellow, in deep pots well drained, in a compost of light loam and leaf-mould and a little old hot-bed stuff, the bulbs put low to allow a liberal top-dressing when they have made a little growth, as they have stem-roots. They should then be put in a cold frame and kept just safe from frost. After the top dressing has been applied, and while the Lilies are growing strongly, a little weak liquid manure will help them.

LILIUM HENRYI (Japan), *Archelirion*

This, though a Lily of recent introduction, promises to be an easily grown garden plant, for it has done well in almost all the cases we have heard of where it has had a fair trial.

It is a handsome thing, the flower being much like that of a large *L. speciosum*, but of a strong and yet soft orange colour. To see the plant growing it impresses one with a feeling of vigour and well-being. When established it will rise to a height of six feet, and bear

Lilium Henryi in a cottage garden. ". . . a handsome thing. . . of a strong and yet soft colour. To see the plant growing it impresses one with a feeling of vigour and well-being."

as many as twenty flowers. In short, though we have known it but a short time, it can be confidently recommended.   It must be planted deep, as it forms an unusually strong mass of stem-roots.

Good reports of it come from peaty loam in Wigtonshire, light loam in Nottinghamshire, heavy loam in Carnarvonshire, light, dry soil in Kent, red loam in Devon, and yellow loam in Sussex. We had only one report of it where it was not completely successful, from a hungry gravel in Middlesex.

CHAPTER V

SUB-GENUS IV
LILIUM PHILADELPHICUM (North America),
Isolirion

A RATHER small and pretty Lily, though not so important as others of this group; cup-shaped, orange spotted, and brighter coloured to the ends of the petals. About three feet high. It likes a cool, damp place in peat. A correspondent in the State of Connecticut speaks of collecting them by grassy roadsides, and we hear of them also in dry woods. The bulbs are very small.

LILIUM CONCOLOR (China), *Isolirion*

One of the best dwarf Lilies, scarlet with dark spots. This is undoubtedly a beautiful small Lily, but it seems to be but little cultivated. It is probably a plant for careful culture in a choice spot in the rock-garden or its near neighbourhood. The stem, which is eighteen inches to two feet high, bears five or six of the scarlet cup-shaped flowers. It likes the usual Lily soil of light loam and leaf-mould, though we hear of it doing well in a peat bed in Northumberland.

LILIUM CORIDION (Japan), *Isolirion*

A very pretty Lily, with solitary flowers of a bright yellow colour, suited for the rock-garden, as it is a small growing kind.

LILIUM CROCEUM, BULBIFERUM OR UMBEL-LATUM (ALPINE REGIONS OF EUROPE), *Isolirion*

THE ORANGE LILY

There is little that need be said about this glorious flower except that it will succeed in almost any garden. It is in fact the most easily grown of all Lilies, doing well even in the heart of London, while thankful for any reasonably good garden treatment.

It increases fast at the bulb and should be divided every few years.

It is a type of the upright open-cupped Lilies of orange and nearly red colouring which is represented in other parts of the world by Lilies of somewhat the same form. Thus it is nearly allied to *L. davuricum* of Siberia, to *L. elegans* of Japan and to *L. Catesbæi* of North America, though none of these can approach it in vigour ; especially as it is so old a garden plant that it has developed into some very strong varieties, some of which rise to a height of seven feet.

It is a flower for the sunny garden border, carrying its grand deep orange cups for nearly three weeks, and its deep green, closely-leafed stems throughout the summer. It will also do well among shrubs in half shade ; indeed it is so hardy and accommodating that there is scarcely any kind of garden space in which it will refuse to grow.

The varieties that bear bulbils in the axils of the leaves can be increased by growing on these little bulbs.

LILIUM CROCEUM ; STRONG ORANGE COLOUR, (*Three inches across.*)

LILIUM ELEGANS=THUNBERGIANUM VAR. ORANGE QUEEN.
COLOUR APRICOT WITH ROSY-BROWN ANTHERS
(*Width Five inches.*)

LILIUM ELEGANS = THUNBERGIANUM. UPPER FLOWER VAR. VAN
HOUTTEI (CRIMSON); LOWER VAR. ALICE WILSON, YELLOW.
ANTHERS, RED BROWN (*Width Five inches.*)

LILIUM CATESBÆI (North America), *Isolirion*

Another of the cup-shaped Lilies, bearing orange-red spotted flowers on slender stems one to two feet high. Like others of the smaller Lilies this is perhaps undeservedly neglected. Each of them has some special character that fits it for some garden use, though probably they are, in gardens generally, less thought of because they are smaller and a little more difficult than the easily grown, bold, and beautiful *L. croceum*. We should advise these Lilies to be used in connection with the rock-garden. Rock-gardens, even when well arranged and well planted, often have a monotony of aspect that might be just redeemed by some such bold departure from the general form of their occupants as would be secured by the upright form of Lilies.

LILIUM DAVURICUM (Siberia), *Isolirion*

This is a good garden Lily and may be regarded as a small *croceum*, with which it is often confounded. It is said to be identical with *L. pennsylvanicum*. The stem is rather slender and from two to three feet high.

LILIUM ELEGANS, syn. THUNBERGIANUM (Japan), *Isolirion*

An admirable short-growing Lily with large upright flowers ; an excellent plant for the rock-garden where a large, dwarf, brilliant flower is needed. It likes

LILIUM BATEMANNIÆ; DEEP ORANGE RED, (Four inches wide.)

a light soil of the usual Lily compost of light loam, peat, and leaf-mould.

There are many varieties of this excellent Lily, varying in colour from pale lemon-yellow to the colour of a rich orange-brown Wallflower, and embracing various tints of orange to almost red and soft apricot and approaching crimson. Copious lists may be found in the catalogues of the best trade growers. All the varieties are beautiful and desirable in the garden.

LILIUM BATEMANNIÆ (JAPAN); possibly a hybrid.
Isolirion

A good garden Lily, brought out by the well-known firm of Lily growers, Messrs Wallace of Colchester. It has unspotted flowers of an even apricot colour. The stems rise about four feet. It is not of difficult cultivation, doing well in ordinary good garden soil. It should be planted rather deep, as it makes roots from the stem.

LILIUM BOLANDERI (One-and-a-half inches) ROSY SCARLET.
L. MARITIMUM (Two inches) ; SCARLET, DARK SPOTTED.
L. PARDALINUM LUTEUM, YELLOW SPOTTED
CHOCOLATE (Three-and-a-half inches.)

LILIUM CANADENSE. YELLOW TO DEEP ORANGE : (Three inches wide.)

CHAPTER VI

SUB-GENUS V

LILIUM CANADENSE (Canada)
L. ROEZLI (California)
L. PARDALINUM (California) } *Martagon*
L. SUPERBUM (Georgia)

FOR garden purposes it is convenient to consider these Lilies together, as they all like moist peat or very light loam in thin woodland. They are in fact related Lilies, agreeing not only in their place in our garden, but in their general character of carrying at or near the top of the stem rather long-stalked flowers, and (all but *L. Roezli*) having the leaves in whorls. They are somewhat alike also in the shape of the root, which, instead of having the form of a more or less compact scaly bulb, becomes a scaly rhizome.

L. canadense is about three feet high, with hanging flowers from one to several in number, on longish stalks. It varies in colour, being yellow in some cases, while in others it is anything from that to a rather pale orange-reddish tint. It is one of the least turn-cap-shaped flowers of the Martagon group, being almost bell-shaped, with the ends of the petals only very slightly turned back. The flowers are handsomely spotted inside. As the plant becomes established the number of flowers increases.

Lilium Roezli is about the same height; in this the leaves are not in whorls. It has bright orange flowers from one to nine or ten in a corymb.

L. superbum. This is the largest Lily of the group, rising to a height of as much as ten feet in suitable conditions of moist peat and woodland shelter. A strong stem will carry a large number, thirty or more, of its handsome flowers, whose colour may be described as a rosy or crimson-orange or orange-crimson.

L. pardalinum. A fine Lily, rising to a height of seven feet, with deep orange flowers with purple spots in the throat. The stems carry from twenty to thirty flowers at the top, on rather long stalks. There are several varieties, differing in stature and colour of bloom.

Those who had the privilege, some years ago, of seeing these swamp Lilies at Mr. Wilson's wood garden at Wisley, when they were being tested for use in English gardens, will remember the astonishment that was produced by their size and vigour and beautiful effect in damp woodland.

LILIUM HUMBOLDTII (California), *Martagon*

A fine Lily, four to five feet high, bearing a large number of flowers in a wide-spread panicle. The individual blooms are well turned back and are of a deep yellow colour richly spotted with purple. There are some good garden varieties. It need not be planted so deeply as some Lilies, for, like the Martagons in general, it makes no stem roots; but the soil must be deep, for the roots go straight down.

LILIUM PARDALINUM; FLOWERS ORANGE AND RED, (Three ins across.)

LILIUM SUPERBUM; FLOWERS ORANGE AND ORANGE RED,
(*Three inches across.*)

LILIUM COLUMBIANUM

is much like a small *L. Humboldtii.*

LILIUM HANSONI (JAPAN), *Martagon*

A beautiful orange Lily, bearing a number of flowers on the top of a stem about three and a half feet high; they are heavily spotted with purple towards the centre. The flowers of this Lily, though reflexed, are not curled-in as is usual with most of the Martagon group. It is a Lily that should be more generally known and grown. It does well in pots.

LILIUM LEICHTLINI (JAPAN), *Martagon*

A beautiful pale lemon-coloured Lily, marked inside with purple, on stems about three feet high. This is not a plant for every garden, but for the careful amateur, one of whom advises that it should be grown in sandy loam lightened with peat. One reason for failure in gardens may be that it comes out of the ground early and therefore needs protection from spring frosts. It is not a good Lily for pots, because, like *L. neilgherrense,* the flower-stem travels away from the bulb horizontally before rising.

LILIUM MARTAGON (EUROPE, ASIA), *Martagon*
MARTAGON LILY

A very old garden flower, and, though not bright of colour, always a favourite; indeed one can scarcely think of an old English garden without the dull purple

WHITE MARTAGON IN A GARDEN BORDER.

PART OF A SPIKE OF L. SZOVITSIANUM; CITRON YELLOW; ORANGE
SCARLET ANTHERS, (Four inches wide)

"*If it were a question of preparing a place for the purest pleasure in the enjoyment of Lily beauty it might be best arranged in some cool, sheltered leafy place; some shady bay in woodland close to, though removed from the garden proper.*" Lilium Pardalinum.

Martagon Lilies. The same distinctive form, also commonly known as turn-cap and turk's-cap, runs through the allied Lilies of many countries, for we have it in the scarlet *pomponium* of northern Italy and the yellow Lily of the Pyrenees, in *chalcedonicum* of Greece and Asia Minor, in *tenuifolium* of Siberia, in *superbum* and *Humboldtii* of the United States; all these, with several others, belonging to the great Martagon group.

Of Martagons proper there are some distinct varieties. *M. dalmaticum* is a strong growing kind with flowers of varying shades of purple; *M. d. Catani* has the flower very dark, almost purple-black or crimson-black; but the greatest treasure is the white, a flower of rare beauty. They like loamy soil, in which they will do almost in any position, but they are finest in cool and damp places, though they do not flourish in the very coldest of our soils and climates. Martagons make no stem roots, rooting only from the bulb. They need not therefore be planted deep.

LILIUM MONADELPHUM SZOVITSIANUM, syn. COLCHICUM (Caucasus), *Martagon*

This Lily is so commonly called *szovitsianum* that it will be so called throughout this handbook. A grand garden Lily, with bright black-spotted lemon-yellow flowers on strong, rather thick stems, four to five feet high. The type, *L. monadelphum*, is also a good thing, but as *L. m. szovitsianum* is just a good shade better it is named in preference as a garden flower. It is rather strongly scented.

LILIUM TENUIFOLIUM; SCARLET, NEARLY LIFE SIZE *(see page 100)*

LILIUM PYRENAICUM (PYRENEES), *Martagon*

This yellow Lily is often found in cottage gardens. No Lily is more easily grown, but of all its kind it is perhaps the least desirable, for among Lilies it is not of much beauty, and it has a strong faint dis-agreeable smell which makes it unwelcome in most gardens. The stems are about eighteen inches high with some ten flowers on each.

LILIUM CARNIOLICUM (SOUTH-EASTERN EUROPE), *Martagon*

A bright turn-cap Lily, something like *chalcedonicum*, in colour varying from orange to scarlet. The stems are from two to three feet high. We hear of it doing well in strong clay in Northumberland.

LILIUM POLYPHYLLUM (WESTERN HIMALAYAS), *Martagon*

This pretty Lily is not always easy to obtain, but if a better supply were imported, or our growers are able to increase it, it should prove a good plant for our gardens. The white or pale yellow sweet-scented flower is marked with violet, and.is in a loose cluster of four to six, on a stem from two to five feet high. We hear of it doing well in North Wales, where it is perfectly hardy; good drainage and general good management no doubt account for this, for though it will bear frost it is known to be impatient of winter wet.

In its Indian home it grows in gravel and decayed

vegetable soil on northern slopes; some growers have thought it needs moisture, but Mr. Wilson has flowered it well on a rather dry loamy mound.

LILIUM TESTACEUM, syn. L. EXCELSUM (Hybrid),
Martagon

THE NANKEEN LILY

The beautiful Nankeen Lily is one of the very best of its kind. It is not only of charming form and colour, but it is singularly graceful, and the deep mystery of its origin adds to the interest of a plant which has already every merit that can be desired in a garden flower. It is supposed to be a hybrid between *candidum* and one of the scarlet Martagons, either *pomponium* or *chalcedonicum*. The flower is distinctly of the Martagon shape, and it resembles *candidum* in the disposal of the leaves on the stem and in a certain grace of habit and way of swaying to light airs of wind, and in the fact that it is one of the earliest of Lilies to push up out of the ground.

It is said that it has never been found wild. But whatever may be its origin or history it is a lovely Lily for our gardens. The name Nankeen Lily is only an approximate description of the colour of the flower, for whereas nankeen is used as a colour word to describe a kind of clear though rather pale washed-out wash-leather colour, there is a tender warmth in addition that must be allowed for in thinking of the colour of this charming Lily.

It is beautiful in every kind of garden use, though

LILIUM TESTACEUM ; WARM NANKEEN COLOUR ; (Two-and-a-half inches wide.)

LILIUM CHALCEDONICUM (SCARLET MARTAGON), SCARLET.
(Two-and a-half inches across.)

from the tenderness of colouring it loses by being in the mixed border among brighter flowers.

It is perhaps best seen in groups among pale greenery of Fern or *Funkia* and backed by shrubs, or in a fringe of garden woodland, though how good it is in the mass in bold plantings may be seen by the illustration showing it in quantity in a celebrated Essex garden.

In the good loamy soil that it likes it will grow seven feet high, but it is perhaps best at a height of from five to six feet. It makes no stem roots and therefore does not need deep planting.

LILIUM CHALCEDONICUM (Greece and Asia Minor), *Martagon*

Scarlet Martagon

One of the brightest of our summer flowers is the scarlet Martagon or scarlet Turn-cap. Its stiff and yet graceful stem bears its cluster of brilliant bloom at the top, while the leaves, larger and longer below, diminish as they rise and clothe the stem very prettily. It has been in our gardens a little over a hundred years. It likes a loamy soil, and as it makes root only from the bulbs need not be planted deep.

L. chalcedonicum will bear drought better than most Lilies, as it comes from near mountain tops of ranges in Eastern Europe and Western Asia. It does not do very much the first year after planting. Parkinson calls it the Red Lily of Constantinople.

LILIUM POMPONIUM (Northern Italy), *Martagon*

A brilliant red turn-cap, much like *chalcedonicum,* but the head of the flowers rather more loosely arranged. It grows three feet high and is of easy culture.

LILIUM TENUIFOLIUM (Siberia), *Martagon*

A small slender-growing Lily, not over a foot high, with bright scarlet flowers. A pretty little plant, a gem for the rock-garden, but probably only successful in the hands of the careful amateur. We hear from Mr. Max Leichtlin that a new stock should constantly be grown from seed. It produces its greatest number of flowers—six to ten—in its fourth year, ripens plenty of seed and then dies away by degrees.

SUB-GENUS VI

The sixth sub-genus, *Notholirion,* contains two plants, *L. Hookeri* and *L. roseum,* which appear to be a link between the Lilies and the Fritillaries. As they are not generally known, and, compared with the distinct Lilies, are not of much importance in our gardens, they are not here described.

LILIUM POMPONIUM ; SCARLET ; (Two inches across.)

LILIUM TESTACEUM IN THE WILD GARDEN.

CHAPTER VII

SOME BEAUTIFUL WAYS OF GROWING LILIES

THE greater number of the Lilies look their best when seen among shrubs and green growths of handsome foliage. Their forms are so distinct as well as beautiful that they are much best in separate groups among quiet greenery—not combined with other flowers. This general rule is offered for consideration as applicable to Lilies of white, pink, lemon-yellow, or other tender colourings ; not so much to those that have scarlet and orange flowers. These are admirable in combination with many other garden flowers in the mixed border and various garden spaces. The White Lily, also, which loves sunlight, is so old a garden flower, and seems so naturally to accompany the Cabbage Roses and late Dutch Honeysuckle and other old garden flowers of the early days of July, that one must allow that its place in our gardens is in combination with the other old favourites.

But if it were a question of preparing a place for the purest pleasure in the enjoyment of Lily beauty it might be best arranged in some cool, sheltered, leafy place ; some shady bay in woodland close to, though removed from, the garden proper. It should be in a place that was fairly moist yet well drained, where the Lilies would rise from ground rather thickly grouped with hardy Ferns and low bushes and plants of good foliage. Mr. R. W. Wallace of Colchester, in his highly instructive paper read at the meeting of the Royal Horticultural Society on July 17, 1900, and published in that Society's Journal, says : " An ideal spot for Lilies would be an open forest glade with a small stream running through it, near the banks of which the North American peat and moisture-loving Lilies would flourish ; and higher up, away from the water, clumps of *auratum, washingtonianum, Humboldti, giganteum,* and all our finest species, would readily grow."

If Lilies were planted in such a place, one kind at a time in fair quantity, we should be better able to appreciate their beauty and their dignity than when they are crowded among numbers of other flowers in the garden borders.

The value of rather close shelter of tree and bush can scarcely be overrated, for the outlying branches of the near bushes protect young Lily growths from the late frosts that are so harmful, and the encircling trees, not near enough to rob at the root or overhang at the top, but so near as to afford passing shade and to stop all violence of wind, give just the protection that suits them best.

It is a great advantage to have the Lilies in so well sheltered a place that they need not be staked, for staking deprives the plant of one of its beautiful ways, that of swaying to the movement of the air. It would scarcely be believed by any one who had not watched

LILIUM GIGANTEUM IN WOODLAND.

WHITE LILY AND SUNDIAL.

LILIUM JAPONICUM BROWNII IN A FIR WOOD AT MR. WILSON'S.

LILIUM TESTACEUM IN THE GARDEN LANDSCAPE.

them unstaked, how variously and diversely graceful are the natural movements of Lilies. If they are tied up to stakes all this is necessarily lost, as is also the naturally dignified and yet dainty poise of the whole plant.

Where the Lily groups have penetrated into true woodland, a background of wild Bracken is the best that can be. As the Lily ground approaches the garden, clumps of Solomon's Seal would be admissible, and that good woodland plant of allied character, *Smilacina racemosa*, and plenty of our best hardy Ferns, Male Fern, Lady Fern, Dilated Shield Fern, and Osmunda, and some of the fine hardy American Ferns, among them also some of the Osmundas, with Onoclea and *Adiantum pedatum*.

Where the Lilies actually join the garden ground, no plant suits them so well as the bold-leaved *Funkia grandiflora*. *Liliums longifolium, Brownii, Krameri,* and *speciosum* are specially thankful for this association. The *Funkia* also enjoys partial shade, for though it flowers best in sun, yet the leaves burn in its fiercest heat. No one would ever regret a good planting of *Lilium longifolium*, Lady Fern, and *Funkia*. *Funkia grandiflora* is the best of the family, because the leaves are of the fresh, light, yellow-green colour that is so becoming to white and tender-coloured flowers.

Sometimes, where there is a permanent group of Lilies in a place where the roots of trees would be likely to rob a special compost, it is a good plan, as has been practised at Mr. Wilson's, to plant the Lilies in a sunk tub.

A WELL GROWN GROUP OF LILIUM TESTACEUM.

THE WHITE LILY IN A COTTAGE GARDEN.

CHAPTER VIII

LILIES IN THE ROCK-GARDEN

WHEN thinking of plants suitable for the rock-garden, one does not always take Lilies into consideration, and yet some of the very best effects may be obtained by their use.

In a rock-garden of large extent and bold features there is no reason why nearly all but the very largest Lilies should not be planted ; but even in smaller places the bold and graceful upright Lily-form may often redeem a rock-garden from the over-squatness of treatment so often seen.   Moreover, when one thinks of a delicate and brilliant gem like *tenuifolium*, with its scarlet turn-cap flower coming, as it does, so early in the Lily season ; of the small-growing orange-coloured *philadelphicum ;* of the many gorgeous and tender-coloured varieties of *elegans* (*thunbergianum*), with their small stature and large bloom ; of *concolor* and *coridion*, two charming dwarf kinds ; of the lovely pink *rubellum*—one sees that Lilies in the rock-garden should by no means be neglected.   Several of the species are from rocky lands, and the complete drainage of the upper portions of the rock-garden is greatly in their favour.

LILIUM KRAMERI IN THE ROCK GARDEN.

*LILIUM LONGIFLORUM IN POTS, ARRANGED WITH FUNKIAS,
CANNAS, ETC., IN THE ANGLE OF A PAVED GARDEN COURT.*

CHAPTER IX

LILIES IN POTS IN OUTDOOR GROUPS

IN a newly made garden, especially if it includes architectural accessories, whether of refined and classical character or roughly built of some local stone, a great addition to the garden's beauty and delightfulness is made by properly considered and designed places for the standing of groups of plants in pots.

It would be the care of the designer so to draw his plans that these spaces would not look hungry or naked in winter, while in summer the plants should appear to be occupying their own proper place, and not be there as interlopers or clumsy afterthoughts. The great advance of late years in the use of important plants, such as Lilies and Cannas, makes the consideration of such a department in garden design a necessity. In many cases it may be a sunk bed in the stone-work. Where it is to contain some of the strongest growing plants, such as the older kinds of Cannas of large stature, a bed may be best, but just now it is the arrangement of plants in pots that is being considered. Sheltered spots in connection with walled garden courts are about the best places for such groups, and Lilies will be the most important of the plants used.

For this purpose the best kinds are *longiflorum, candidum, auratum, Krameri,* and *speciosum.* In such groupings nothing is more important, as a suitable setting to the Lilies, than to have a good supply of the best foliage, also in pots. For this the plants most to be recommended are *Funkia grandiflora,* and hardy Ferns as advised for the woodland groups, Male Fern, Lady Fern, and Dilated Shield Fern. All these are grown out of doors in a sheltered place, having been potted in October. The plants take two years to come to their best, and will stand in the pots three or four years, after which they are thankful for a shift. The only indoor plants used with these are *Aspidistras,* which are much benefited by the outdoor treatment.

There is no reason why any other plants of good green foliage that may be liked should not be used, but it is convenient to describe an arrangement that has been actually done, and found to answer so well that for three or four years it has remained unchanged.

The groups of green are put out in the first week of June. In the place in question there is no convenience for bringing on early batches of *Lilium longiflorum,* so that the first flower effect is given by pots of white Gladiolus (the Bride), and some Hydrangeas, white and pink. But in the shady place all white and tender-coloured flowers look well, while all gain immensely from being placed in the ample groundwork of cool greenery of only a few kinds of plants, and these not mixed up, but easily grouped.

A very simple grouping such as this of a few green

"In a garden. . . . whether of refined and classical character or roughly built of some local stone, a great addition to the garden's beauty and delightfulness is made by properly considered and designed places for the standing of groups of plants in pots. . . . Sheltered spots. . . are about the best places for such groups, and Lilies will be the most important of the plants used." *Lilium Speciosum.*

things and a few kinds of Lilies, is beautiful beyond comparison with a placing of a miscellaneous collection of potted flowers. A sunny place would be differently treated, with other plants, but it is doubtful if any would be so pictorially satisfactory as the cool, shaded place, with its white or tender-coloured Lilies, and their amply sufficient groundwork of handsome greenery.

CHAPTER X

LILIES AS CUT FLOWERS

THERE can be no two opinions about the beauty of Lilies as ·cut flowers for the house. The only objection that can be made to them in this use is that some have too strong a scent. This is especially the case with *auratums*, which are therefore more suitable for a hall or entrance than for an actual sitting-room. The lovely *candidum* is also rather strong in a room, though to many the scent is so welcome, as one of the sweet smells of high summer-tide, that it is liked in the sitting-room as well as in the garden. No possible objection on this account can be raised against *longiflorum* or *speciosum*, two of the very best room Lilies, whether cut or in pots. When arranged as cut flowers their nobility of aspect necessarily restricts the choice of kinds of foliage to be put with them. Nothing small or petty can come near these Lilies ; the leafage that is put with them must have some kind of dignity of its own. *Lilium longiflorum* may have enough of its own foliage, but if any is added it should be something of the same dark colouring and high polish, such as *Magnolia grandiflora*, of which a well-grown tree can always spare a branch or two, or a bough of a

"It is a great advantage to have the Lilies in . . . a place that they need not be staked, for staking deprives the plant of one of its beautiful ways, that of swaying to the movement of the air. . . [for] how variously and diversely graceful are the natural movements of Lilies."

dark-leaved green *Aucuba*, or *Acanthus latifolius* prepared by a bath of some hours in a tank or tub.

L. speciosum and its varieties admit of much more variety in the choice of foliage. If there are strong growing examples of *Magnolia conspicua*, some of their summer shoots of handsome pale leaves, probably two feet long, can well be spared; if the tree is against a wall a good quantity will be available. It is well worth keeping in the reserve garden a patch of Maize and a little of the variegated kind, on purpose for cutting to go with Lilies and Gladiolus and other important summer and autumn flowers. If the first shoots of the Maize are cut when they are three feet high, it will push again from the base and give a number of useful shoots of graceful greenery for the autumn. It should be remembered that, like so many of the Lilies, Maize also makes stem roots, so that it should be planted at the bottom of a depression or in a trench, and given a good dressing of compost to fill up to the level when the stem roots begin to show.

Leaves of *Funkia grandiflora* are also delightful with these Lilies ; a good breadth should be grown for cutting, in a half-shaded place well guarded from slugs ; the leaves burn in the sun. Fronds of hardy Ferns, especially Lady Fern, are also good, but they should be prepared by a bath of some hours.

The tender pink and rosy colouring of *L. speciosum* are also beautiful with grey foliage. Of this the grandest will be leaves of Globe Artichoke or Cardoon. A reserve of these in full sunlight should also be

LILIUM KRAMERI WITH FOLIAGE OF GREEN AUCUBA.

THE NANKEEN LILY WITH MAIZE FOLIAGE.

kept for cutting ; the flower stems should be cut
out in order to insure a succession of the leaves.
These must also be immersed in the tank to prepare
them to stand well in water.

Many of the orange-coloured Lilies are also good
in rooms ; *croceum* and *tigrinum* being among the
most useful. They are generally well enough fur-
nished with leaves to do without addition, and their
fine forms are so best seen ; the stiffness of the
laterally directed flower stalks of the Tiger Lily
makes it very easy to arrange, one flower support-
ing another.

CHAPTER XI

LILIES FOR TOWN GARDENS

THERE is no better town plant than the grand *Lilium croceum*. It seems to bear its well-filled heads of great orange cups as willingly in a London square as in a country garden, while the leaves show by their deep green colour, and the whole plant by its robust health and vigour, how little it cares about those conditions of town life that are so surely fatal to many plants. Indeed nearly all the Lilies named in the chapter on the easiest grown garden Lilies will do well in towns. They comprise—

L. auratum	*L. Humboldti*
L. Brownii	*L. longiflorum*
L. candidum	*L. pardalinum*
L. chalcedonicum	*L. pyrenaicum*
L. croceum	*L. testaceum*
L. davuricum	*L. tigrinum*
L. elegans	

CHAPTER XII

LILIES FOR DIFFERENT SOILS

IT has been observed by some of our best amateurs that it is not usual for more than four or five kinds of Lilies to do well in the ordinary soil of any one garden. This is scarcely to be wondered at when one thinks of the enormous geographical distribution of these plants. All the known Lilies are natives of the northern hemisphere, and virtually within the temperate zone ; any that occur within the Tropic of Cancer are in mountainous places at an elevation of some thousands of feet. They extend from Japan in the east to the western States of America, and as they grow in every variety of soil and situation it stands to reason that the conditions offered by any one garden are not likely to suit a large number of species.

But as gardening consists not only in doing what is easiest but also in taking pains to suit plants with what they want, by learning what are the needs of the Lilies that may be most admired by any individual amateur they may generally be made to succeed.

Still it will be reasonable to give the preference to the Lilies that will be favoured by the soil of the garden, and the following list will approximately show the likings of the kinds we have to deal with.

Good average garden soil or a mixture of medium loam and leaf soil will suit

Batemanniæ	*longiflorum*
candidum	*Martagon*
chalcedonicum	*pyrenaicum*
concolor	*pomponium*
croceum	*speciosum*
coridion	*szovitsianum*
elegans	*tenuifolium*
Hansoni	*testaceum*
Henryi	*tigrinum*

These therefore may be regarded as Lilies for every garden except those that are of a very light sandy peat, and even in these *croceum, tigrinum, Henryi, Brownii,* and *rubellum* will do very well.

The Lilies that prefer a stiffer soil and will do in it as well as in the average soil are :—

candidum	* *neilgherrense*
chalcedonicum	* *nepalense*
giganteum	*pomponium*
Humboldti	*szovitsianum*
Krameri	* *sulphureum*
Leichtlini	*testaceum*
* *Lowi*	*washingtonianum*
Martagon	

Those that like peat and moisture are :—

canadense	*philadelphicum*
Grayi	*superbum*
pardalinum	*Wallacei*
Parryi	*auratum*

* These are tender and require house culture, except in quite the south of England.

CHAPTER XIII

HOW LILIES DO IN DIFFERENT PARTS OF ENGLAND

THE Lilies that do generally well in gardens having been considered in the last chapter are therefore omitted from this ; their cultural requirements are given under their separate names, and also in the chapter referred to ; those also known to do well with certain treatment or in certain natural conditions, such as *L. giganteum*, do not appear here. The tender Indian Lilies, those that are best in greenhouse treatment, are also excluded, and will be found in their place. In the following the kinds are placed alphabetically :—

L. Batemanniæ.

> Failure in strong loam in Northumberland, in the same garden doing well in peat.
> Well in red loam in South Devon.
> Well in sandstone and peat in South Devon.

The best reports of this Lily come from Devonshire. We therefore assume that it is somewhat tender.

L. Brownii.

> Fairly well in heavy loam in Cumberland.
> Well in strong loam in Northumberland.

Very well in light soil (Hastings sand) in Kent.

Fairly well in alluvial soil, deep and light, apt to dry ; in Dublin.

Fairly well in light sandy loam on chalk in Surrey.

Failure in green sand on stony soil in Radnorshire.

Well in sandy peat in Kircudbrightshire.

Fairly well in light loam in Nottinghamshire.

Well in light dry soil, subsoil gravel, in Warwickshire.

Very well in loam and peat in Norfolk.

Well in red sandstone and peat in South Devon.

Well in loam in Surrey.

Well in heavy red loam in South Devon.

L. canadense.

Well spoken of in moist, peaty soils.

L. davuricum.

Well in peat and loam in Devon.

Very well in a gravelly, dry garden in Middlesex.

L. elegans = *thunbergianum.*

Well in heavy red loam in South Devon.

Well in red sandstone and peat in South Devon.

Well in red loam in South Devon.

Well in sandy peat and gravel in Kirkcudbrightshire.

Well in alluvial soil in Dublin.

Well in strong loam on clay in Northumberland.

L. Hansoni.

Well in peaty sand and loam in Devon.
Very well in a dry, gravelly garden in Middlesex.
Well in strong loam on clay in Northumberland.
Well in sandy loam on gravel in Durham.
Well in red loam in South Devon.
Well in loam in Sussex.

Nearly all the reports we have had speak well of this Lily.

L. Humboldti.

Well in peaty loam near the sea in Wigtonshire.

Fairly well in a dry, gravelly garden in Middlesex.

Well in strong loam on clay subsoil in Northumberland ; also well in a peat bed in the same garden.

Well in disintegrated syenite with strong loam and peat in Worcestershire.

Well in red loam in South Devon.

Failure in loam in Surrey.

Grand in heavy red loam in South Devon.

Well in loam in Sussex.

These reports should be encouraging to the use of this handsome Lily.

L. Krameri.

Very well in heavy yellow clay in Sussex.
Failure outside in sandy peat in Dumfriesshire.
Fairly well in sandy soil in Shropshire.

Very well in sandy loam on chalk subsoil in
Surrey.

Very well in peaty loam in Wigtonshire.

Unequal in alluvial soil (apt to dry) in Dublin.

Well in peat (soil red sandstone) in South
Devon.

Failure in loam in Surrey.

The reports of this Lily vary considerably, but it is
so beautiful that we advise amateurs to give it a good
trial.

L. Leichtlini.

Only two reports of this graceful Lily came in,
one doubtful and one favourable.

L. longiflorum.

Out of fourteen reports continued success in
garden culture was only mentioned in four
cases, others being moderate, and some
failures. It is not a plant that can be expected to grow on and increase in English
gardens, but it is imported in such vast
quantities, and brought to our doors at so
cheap a rate, that its popularity is not likely
to wane, while as a pot Lily it is one of the
most valuable.

L. pardalinum.

Of this we had seventeen notices, of which a
few are as follows :—

Well in strong loam in Northumberland.

Well in peat, sand, and loam in Devon.

Well in stiff calcareous soil on clay subsoil in Hampshire.

Well in moist alluvial soil in Dublin.

Well in disintegrated syenite and strong loam in Worcestershire.

Well in sandy loam and gravel in Durham.

Well in disintegrated red sandstone and peat in South Devon.

Very well in heavy red loam and leaf soil in South Devon.

Well in loam in Sussex.

These reports show the wonderful adaptability of this Lily to a variety of soil, and therefore indicates that we may consider it a Lily for all English gardens.

L. Parryi.

Two successes, three doubtful cases, and one failure are recorded against this pretty Californian Lily, but probably it is from its not being generally known that it should be grown in moist peat. Since these reports came in we have had a most favourable account of it from an amateur in Kent.

L. philadelphicum.

Only mentioned once in the reports received, describing it as short-lived.

L. rubellum.

This beautiful new Lily is extremely well spoken of wherever it has had a fair trial in sandy or peaty soils.

L. speciosum.

> Well in sandy peat and loam in Kent.
>
> Well in disintegrated syenite, peat, and loam in Worcestershire.
>
> Well in heavy loam and granite in Carnarvonshire.
>
> Well in disintegrated red sandstone and peat in South Devon.
>
> Well in loam in Surrey.
>
> Fairly in heavy red loam in South Devon.

There are other less satisfactory reports of this lovely Lily in its many varieties, but on the whole they are encouraging to use it as a garden plant as well as a pot plant.

L. superbum.

> This Lily is so much like *pardalinum* in its needs that we need hardly repeat the general praise of its well doing, especially in moist peat in a partly shaded place.

L. tenuifolium.

> This small Siberian Lily is not much cultivated, and our reports said but little of it ; but we find it does well in warm, sandy soil. The stock should be renewed from seed.

L. washingtonianum.

> Uncertain on oolite limestone in Gloucestershire.

Well in loam and sand in Norfolk.

Well in strong loam on clay subsoil in North-umberland.

L. Wallacei.

Is reported only once, but then as doing well.

CHAPTER XIV

IMPORTED AND HOME-GROWN LILIES

THERE are two ways of buying Lilies; the safe and sure way of having home-grown bulbs from a house of good repute, and the risky way of buying imported ones at auction sales.

By following the latter course a much larger number of bulbs may be had, but there are likely to be failures. It is a kind of horticultural gambling; the buyer may win a prize of a case of good bulbs at a very cheap rate, or he may draw a blank and be so much the loser.

If on receiving a case of imported bulbs they are found to be limp and flabby, they should, before potting or planting, be put for a time into just damp cocoa-fibre, when they will soon plump up. Sometimes they arrive bruised and partly decayed. The worst had better be burnt at once; any that seem worth saving, or have only small blue mouldy patches, may be benefited by being well dusted with powdered charcoal, or treated with dry powdered sulphur, getting the cleansing and fungoid-growth-destroying powder well in between the scales.

It is best not to buy imported *auratums* early in the season; the first consignments often contain bulbs insufficiently ripened. Those that reach England after Christmas are likely to be better.

CHAPTER XV

LILIES AS POT PLANTS

For pot culture the Lilies that do best, and at the same time are the most useful for the decoration of dwelling-house or conservatory, are, *longiflorum*, *candidum*, *auratum*, and *speciosum* among the hardiest and easiest, then *Krameri*, *Brownii*, and the tender Indian kinds, *sulphureum* (*wallichianum*), *odorum*, and *Lowi*.

The compost that will suit most Lilies is a mixture of good loam and peat with a little leaf-mould, in the proportion of two parts fibrous loam, one part fibrous peat with a little leaf-mould and sand. This may be called the stock Lily compost. It may be with advantage varied as follows. For *candidum* rather heavier loam and a little lime rubbish, for *speciosum* heavier loam, for *Krameri*, *Brownii*, *sulphureum*, *odorum*, &c., rather lighter loam, for *longiflorum* rather more manurial matter, but of course well decayed.

Pots for Lilies should be roomy and above all deep, especially for the Lilies that make stem-roots. Out of those named above these will be all but *candidum*. The stem-rooting Lilies are generally potted low in the pot and additional compost is added when the stem-roots appear; this will bear to be a little richer than the compost in which the bulb is first potted.

Lilium longiflorum under glass is apt to be attacked by green fly, crowds of which assemble in the rather closely gathered leaves at the top of the stem when it is half grown. Fumigating should be begun in good time and kept up at intervals. If they are wanted early they must be kept in a moist atmosphere, well watered and often syringed.

For starting the bulbs no way is better than plunging them in a bed of ashes four inches deep over the pots, as is done with Hyacinths; then the pots will be transferred to house or cold frame as they are wanted for use indoors in the earliest months or later in the open.

Those that are for outdoor use can also be potted later. They are kept in a cool frame just safe from frost. When danger from frost is over they are plunged in an ash-bed in the open ground. After the top-dressing, a little weak liquid manure may be given to the *speciosum* varieties and to *longiflorum.*

For the treatment of Lilies in pots after the bloom is over, the supply of water should gradually be decreased—they should be plentifully watered while growing and flowering—until the stems have turned yellow; they are then fresh potted and kept rather dry in the cold frame for the winter.

CHAPTER XVI

DEEP OR SHALLOW PLANTING

THERE are two matters connected with Lily growing whose importance is often overlooked, and to the neglect of which many failures may probably be attributed ; one is the right depth of planting, and the other is neglect in giving due protection from spring frost.

As a rough rule a Lily is planted at a depth represented by three times that of the bulb, except in the case of *L. giganteum,* which is planted barely underground. But Lilies have two ways of throwing out roots. Some of them, including *candidum* and all the *Martagons,* root only at the base of the bulb. But in a great number the bulb makes its first growth by the help of the roots from its base, known as basal roots ; then as soon as the stem begins to rise, it throws out a fresh set from the stem itself, above the point where it comes out of the bulb. These are the roots that feed the later growth of the stem and flowers. It follows that if one of these Lilies is planted only just underground, the stem-roots will push out above ground, and, finding no nourishment, the growth of the plant will be checked. But if these stem-roots are well underground, and their strong growth is further encouraged by the rich mulch that is recommended, and by frequent waterings in dry days of spring and early summer, the

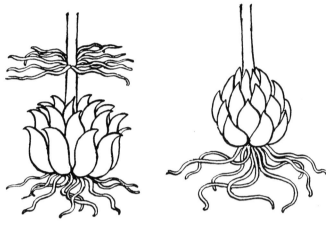

LILY THAT MAKES STEM-ROOTS, SUCH AS L. AURATUM.

THAT MAKE NO STEM-ROOTS, SUCH AS L. CANDIDUM.

stem-roots can do their duty in supplying the stem and flowers with the needful nourishment.

The following is a list of the Lilies that root from the stem as well as from the bulb, and therefore require deep planting ; the names are put alphabetically :—

auratum, including all varieties and the fine Japanese hybrid *L. a. Alexandræ.*
Batemanniæ
Brownii
croceum
Dalhansoni

elegans
Hansoni
Henryi
Krameri
longiflorum
nepalense
speciosum
tigrinum

The following are the Lilies that root from the bulb only, and therefore do not need such deep planting :—

Burbanki	*Humboldti*
canadense	*Martagon*
candidum	*pardalinum*
chalcedonicum	*pomponium*
excelsum	*superbum*
giganteum	*szovitsianum*
Grayi	*washingtonianum*

CHAPTER XVII

PROTECTION FROM SPRING FROSTS

AGAIN remembering that our garden Lilies come from all countries in the northern half of the temperate world, from valleys, mountains, rocky heights, and swamps, we must be prepared for the fact that their young growths pierce the ground at very different dates, and that, though no doubt each Lily in its own place comes out of the ground at the fittest season for its new growth, when we put them into our gardens we cannot suit them with the exact weather and temperature and altitude that they would expect in their own homes.

It follows that most of the Lilies that come early out of the ground will need some kind of protection. The best protection of all is that of growing shrubs, whose branches nearly meet over the spot where the Lily is planted. This is one reason why it is so strongly recommended that *Lilium auratum* and others should be grown through and among Rhododendrons and other shrubs.

The Lilies that like the closest growths around them may be known by having the lower part of the stem more or less bare of leaves, as is the case with *auratum ;* those which, like *candidum,* spire up from a thick leafy mass show that they do not need the shrubby cover ; but for the early growing Lilies it is important that they should be given some shelter from frost. A mulch of short manure, of half-decayed leaves, or of cocoa-fibre is good as a ground protection ; but something is wanted beyond this, for it often happens, when the ground covering only has been provided, that the Lily growth pushes through it while we have yet to fear the late frosts of April and May. Fir boughs, either Scotch or Spruce, are capital for this sheltering, and one of our best Lily amateurs, writing from Kent, says that he has found the branches of *Berberis Aquifolium* give complete success. Even bare boughs, such as old pea sticks, will, as gardeners say, "break the frost," and are much better than nothing. The same helpful amateur has sent these dates as those at which the growth of the following Lilies may be expected :—

Name of Lily.	Date of Appearance.
Lilium longiflorum Takesima	March 8th.
L. auratum platyphyllum	„ 11th.
L. speciosum cruentum	„ 17th.
L. Henryi } *L. Hansoni* }	„ 19th.
L. speciosum album Krætzeri	„ 25th.
L. Brownii	April 12th.
L. excelsum	„ 13th.
L. Parryi } *L. Burbanki* }	„ 20th.
L. szovitsianum } *L. rubellum* }	„ 28th.
L. canadense	May 4th.
L. Batemanniæ (planted this spring)	„ 14th.

CHAPTER XVIII

HYBRID LILIES

CONSIDERING how freely Lilies seed it is rather surprising that it is only of late years that we hear much of the raising of hybrid varieties.

Perhaps it is that the carefully cultivated garden kinds—that is to say, the garden forms of natural species—are so good, that the attempt to mingle the various characters could not produce anything better than we have already. Thus we can scarcely imagine an improvement on the best form of *L. candidum*, or a grander flower than a bold *L. auratum* such as *L. a. platyphyllum*.

It is probable that the efforts of those who are now hybridising Lilies, will end by producing just a few excellent things and a large number of confusing nondescripts, much worse as garden plants than the types from which they are derived.

Still, though it is difficult to imagine it, there may still be potentialities of beauty undeveloped in the Lily family. In support of this there is the lovely *L. testaceum*, said to be a hybrid of *chalcedonicum* and *candidum*, which, while possessing a beauty of its own, clearly shows the relationship to both parents; to *chalcedonicum* in the form of the flower and the faint tinge of its warm colour, to *candidum* in its port and texture of bloom—the resemblance to this parent being perhaps strongest in the half-grown state in the arrangement and carriage of the leaves.

Certainly no one can deny the success of the Japanese natural hybrid of *auratum* and *longiflorum*, if that be, as is supposed, the true parentage of *Lilium Alexandræ*, but then in the Lily world there are not many such possible parents as those two grand species.

L. Burbanki, a hybrid of *L. pardalinum* and *L. washingtonianum*, is well spoken of, and there is reason to believe that Mr. Burbank before long will give the world some good new hybrids. The hybrids of *Martagon*, such as *Marhan (Martagon+Hansoni)*, are without doubt interesting, and have a certain degree of beauty, but the genus Lilium seems to offer a field for the working of better things. It is to be hoped that this industrious and able hybridist or some other enthusiast will work among the white Lilies. The orange yellows, in the *croceum* and *Martagon* groups, are already so numerous, and to the unlearned amateur so confusing, that the best that can be done with them is to derive if possible bold flowers of self colouring rather than a mere series of connecting links between species of secondary importance. It should be remembered that what is wanted in a garden is beautiful flowers rather than many different kinds of flowers. Many a possibly lovely garden is ruined by too great a mixture, and could only be redeemed by the practice

A HYBRID LILY; PARRYI + PARDALINUM, DEEP ORANGE (Flowers,
Three inches across. Raised by an Amateur.)

*LILIUM DALHANSONI; A HYBRID OF MARTAGON DALMATICUM
AND HANSONI. FLOWERS ORANGE BROWN (Two inches across.)*

of severe restraint in the number of kinds of things to be seen at one glance.

A good hybrid Lily has been raised at Kew, named *L. Kewense,* the progeny of *L. Henryi* and a fine form of *L. Brownii.* It is of a creamy buff colour turning nearly white, in general appearance something like a small *auratum.*

A hybridist who could get the grand substance of the tender Indian Lilies into hardy garden plants of good constitution would indeed be a benefactor to horticulture.

CHAPTER XIX

THE LILY DISEASE

THERE is one disappointment that growers of Lilies must occasionally be prepared for, namely, the Lily disease, often taking a form that is known as "spot." In some cases spots of brown decay appear on the leaves, in others decay seizes some part of the half-grown stem as well, as if it had been subjected to a jet of scalding steam, and the stem falls over. Sometimes an almost full-grown stem is attacked at a late stage of its growth and it is able to open one or two flowers, which present a miserable appearance, crowning the whole stem-length of decaying rags of leaves and blemished stalk. Evidence from the best amateurs shows that disease is much more prevalent in imported bulbs than in those that are home grown, and that are therefore stronger and better able to resist its attacks.

In the matter of disease *Lilium candidum* is as mysterious as in its other ways ; for one year a whole row will be in perfect beauty and the next they will be all infected. Its near relative, *testaceum*, is also commonly subject to disease, and of other Lilies *auratum* is one of the most frequent sufferers.

When the disease appears in *candidum* some growers

attribute it to want of proper drainage and therefore stagnant moisture at the root. The best growers agree in saying that this grand Lily *must* have good drainage, and most of them advocate a warm exposure. We do not know whether it suffers from disease in Italy, where it grows so luxuriantly.

With regard to "spot" in *auratum*, the present writer was much struck last year by the fact that among some Lilies among Rhododendrons "spot" appeared among all that were in sun, while those that were shaded escaped. The thought occurred whether it was possible that it was in this case not a disease originating in the plant itself but the direct burning action of the sun intensified by the lens form of drops of wet. There was no question of frost as it was in very hot weather, about the same time when a good many people noticed that leaves of all kinds were burnt and decayed very quickly when a wet dead flower had fallen and rotted on them.

The existence of disease should make growers all the more careful to do the best they can for their Lilies, for if the plant is in a healthy state we may safely assume that it will not be attacked.

Many columns have appeared in *The Garden* on the subject of the disfiguring and mysterious Lily illness ; no certain preventive or remedy has been suggested, but there is strong presumption in favour of the efficacy of spraying with Bordeaux mixture, that great enemy of fungoid attacks ; for the Lily disease is of that nature and is known to science as

Botritis cinerea. The recipe is given below. The beneficial action of sulphur is well known in vegetable as well as animal pathology, as in the treatment of mildew in plants and skin diseases in animals. One observant amateur treated his bulbs after they were dug up by shaking them up in a paper bag with some flowers of sulphur (sulphur in fine powder) so as to get it well in among the scales; he said that the next season the plants did well and showed no sign of disease.

BORDEAUX MIXTURE

Sulphate of copper and fresh quicklime, one pound each. Dissolve the sulphate in a wooden tub and slake the lime in a pail or anything convenient. Pour the lime when slaked into the sulphate solution, and add ten gallons of water; syringe gently with this mixture, and again a week or ten days later.

INDEX

The Antique Collectors' Club

The Antique Collectors' Club has 12,000 members and the monthly journal (not August), sent free to members, discusses in more depth than is normal for a collectors' magazine the type of antiques and art available to collectors. It is the only British antiques magazine which has consistently grown in circulation over the past decade.

The Antique Collectors' Club also publishes a series of books on antique furniture, art reference and horology, together with various standard works connected with arts and antiques. It also publishes a series of practical books, invaluable to collectors, under the general heading of the Price Guide Series (price revision lists published annually).

New titles are being added to the list at the rate of about ten a year. Why not ask for an updated catalogue?

The Antique Collectors' Club
5 Church Street, Woodbridge, Suffolk, England
Telephone 03943 5501

Other books by Gertrude Jekyll published by the Antique Collectors' Club

Garden Ornament
12ins. × 8½ins./30cm × 22cm. 462 pages. 600 black and white illustrations. Garden design in relation to architecture — gates, steps, balustrades, garden houses, dovecotes, pergolas and many other topics are discussed and examples illustrated.

Gardens for Small Country Houses
by Gertrude Jekyll and Sir Lawrence Weaver
11ins. × 8½ins./28cm × 22cm. 260 pages, 387 black and white illustrations. This book is respected by generations of gardeners who continue to find in it inspiration in planning their own gardens, big or small, for the principles the authors expound are both fundamental and practical.

Colour Schemes for the Flower Garden

8½ ins. × 5½ ins./22cm × 14cm. 328 pages, 120 black and white illustrations, 32 in colour. Generally thought to be the author's best book. Her sense of colour, thoughts on 'painting' a garden and imaginative ideas on planting arrangements make this book a joy to read.

Wood and Garden

8½ ins. × 5½ ins./22cm × 14cm. 380 pages, 71 black and white illustrations, 32 in colour. The first book Jekyll wrote takes the reader through her gardening year month by month. Also included are her practical and critical thoughts on the herbaceous garden, woodland, large and small gardens, and other gardening topics.

Home and Garden

8½ ins. × 5½ ins./22cm × 14cm. 373 pages. 53 black and white illustrations, 16 in colour. In this book Gertrude Jekyll introduces us to her life both as gardener and craftswoman, and discusses in detail the building of her home — Munstead Wood designed by Edwin Lutyens.